MAGICAL MEDITATIONS

A GUIDED JOURNAL FOR

Peace, Clarity, and Creativity

12/2021

Ronni,
I hope you have a very Merry Christmas and know that I love you so so much!
Polly

NIKKI VAN DE CAR

illustrations by

PENELOPE DULLAGHAN

RP STUDIO
PHILADELPHIA

RP Studio™
Hachette Book Group
1290 Avenue of the Americas, New York, NY 10104
www.runningpress.com
@Running_Press

Printed in China

First Edition: September 2020

Published by RP Studio, an imprint of Perseus Books, LLC, a subsidiary
of Hachette Book Group, Inc. The RP Studio name and logo is a trademark
of the Hachette Book Group.

The publisher is not responsible for websites (or their content)
that are not owned by the publisher.

Text by Nikki Van De Car
Design by Susan Van Horn

ISBN: 978-0-7624-7089-1

1010

10 9 8 7 6 5 4 3 2 1

INTRODUCTION

YOU HAVE THE POWER TO CREATE YOUR OWN LIFE EXPERIENCE— for while we cannot control what happens to us, we can control how we respond to it. If we experience a moment of frustration, like getting cut off in traffic, we can decide how it will affect us—will we carry that irritation with us? Or will we go on with our day?

This kind of awareness and conscious choice is not easy. It takes practice, but by creating a ritual of journaling, you will discover the inner strength, self-knowledge, support, and yes, magic, you need to live the life you want.

And as you develop this ritual, you will find that your imagination, feminine power, intuition, connections with others, and creativity are more vibrant than they have ever been. You will feel more connected to the women who inspire you, and more importantly, you will feel more connected to yourself.

This is the true magic—to be who we want to be, and to live the life we choose for ourselves.

The moon is a celestial body of mystery, femininity, and creativity. On the night of a full moon, harness its powers. Sit with your journal and a cup of tea. Allow the moonlight to shine on the page, and simply write down any thoughts that come to you. Be free and easy—you can skip punctuation and even grammar, as you simply let your mind flow.

When you wake from a dream, it is tempting go right back to sleep, sometimes even diving back into it. If you can get back into that half-awake lucid dreaming state, go for it! But once you're truly awake, recount your dream in your journal, including any details you can remember. If you find yourself embellishing, that's okay—in fact, it's great! Novels have been written and movies have been created based on dreams. Your subconscious and your imagination love to play together.

_____

_____

_____

_____

_____

_____

_____

_____

_____

_____

_____

_____

_____

_____

_____

_____

_____

What do I want? What makes me happy? What do I have to offer the world? What is the right choice? These questions are frequently at the heart of all our struggles, and in truth, we can never really give them a final answer. We change and evolve, and what is right *right now* may be wrong tomorrow. But it is in the asking that we get to know ourselves, even as we change. What are your answers, today?

Chakra Meditation.

Sit cross-legged on the floor. Align your spine so that your head is over your heart and your heart is over your hips. Visualize your seat reaching toward the earth as the crown of your head reaches toward the sky. Inhale, and imagine Muladhara, your root chakra, spinning with a red light. Exhale. Inhale, and imagine Svadisthana, your sacral chakra, spinning with an orange light. Exhale. Inhale, and imagine Manipura, your solar plexus chakra, spinning with a yellow light. Exhale. Inhale, and imagine Anahata, your heart chakra, spinning with a green light. Exhale. Inhale, and imagine Vishudda, your throat chakra, spinning with a pale blue light. Exhale. Inhale, and imagine Ajna, your third eye chakra, spinning with a deep blue light. Exhale. Inhale, and imagine Svadisthana, your crown chakra, spinning with a violet light. Exhale. Inhale once more, and imagine each of your seven chakras coming into harmony with one another, blending together until you have a solid core of white light running up and down your spine. Stay with this energy for as long as you like, and then ease yourself out of your meditation.

For one full lunar cycle, write down a single word or phrase on this page every day. Don't put too much thought into it—just write down whatever comes to mind. At the end of the cycle, circle any common themes. What have you learned?

_____	_____	_____
_____	_____	_____
_____	_____	_____
_____	_____	_____
_____	_____	_____
_____	_____	_____
_____	_____	_____
_____	_____	_____

Choose two crystals that connect you to your root chakra, like obsidian, hematite, agate, bloodstone, bronzite, or smoky quartz. Sit cross-legged and place a crystal in each of your hip creases. Hold them there for a moment, rubbing and pressing them in gentle circles, stimulating your root chakra. What does Muladhara have to tell you? How can you feel safe and secure?

_____

_____

_____

_____

_____

_____

_____

_____

_____

_____

_____

_____

_____

_____

_____

_____

_____

_____

Choose a crystal that connects you to your sacral chakra, like sunstone, rutilated quartz, carnelian, garnet, ruby, or citrine. Hold it in your palm and place it right over your lower belly, pressing in gently.
Take a deep breath as you push against your hand. What creative energy can you spark from Svadisthana?

_____

_____

_____

_____

_____

_____

_____

_____

_____

_____

_____

_____

_____

_____

_____

_____

_____

_____

_____

Dream Interpretation.

Our dreams can have symbolic meaning. Which of these common dream themes appear when you sleep?

FALLING:
Indicates a major life change.

TEETH FALLING OUT:
Loss of confidence.

BEING CHASED:
You are about to confront whatever has been troubling you.

FLYING:
You are ready to move outside of your usual habits.

ANIMALS:
The part of you that is connected to nature.

MOUNTAINS:
Obstacles that may be in your path.

WATER:
The unconscious mind.

PARALYSIS:
May indicate that you feel you've lost control.

FOOD:
Can mean information or knowledge.

HOUSE:
This can represent your own mind.

Choose a crystal that connects you to your solar plexus chakra, like tiger's eye, pyrite, yellow jasper, peridot, or mookaite. Place it right between your lower ribs, on that firm muscle, and hold it in place. Tighten your core as you breathe against your crystal. Manipura is the source of your personal power, your strength. What are the ways in which you are strong? Sometimes we need to be reminded.

Choose a crystal that connects you to your heart chakra, like rose quartz, morganite, malachite, emerald, or rhodonite. Place it over your heart center, Anahata, and cup your palms tenderly over it. Roll forward a bit, curling in to protect the heart, and then arch back up, shining your heart up to the sky. What do you love? Write down *everything*—your family, your friends, television shows, books, hedgehogs, kittens, rain, sunshine, everything—until you've filled the page entirely.

Choose a crystal that connects you to your throat chakra,
like aquamarine, turquoise, sodalite, or blue lace agate. Place it in
the hollow at the base of your throat, gently holding the stone in place.
Hum a little, so that you can feel the vibration moving through Visuddha.
And now, *speak out*. What have you kept silent?

_____

_____

_____

_____

_____

_____

_____

_____

_____

_____

_____

_____

_____

_____

_____

_____

_____

Grounding Meditation.

Kick off your shoes and sit outside on the grass.
In this meditation, you don't want to disappear from
your experience, but really be *in it*. Feel the grass
tickling at your ankles. Feel the breeze blowing your hair.
Inhale any scents, and listen to any sounds you may hear.
Birds, leaves rustling, cars going by—just take it all in.
Use this time to really experience what it is like
to be alive in the world.

Choose a crystal that connects you to your third eye chakra, like lapis lazuli, azurite, fluorite, fuchsite, lepidolite, sapphire, labradorite, or apophyllite. Place the crystal right on Ajna, just above and between your eyebrows. Close your eyes and sit quietly until the crystal reaches your body temperature. As you wait, pay attention—what do you see? What do you feel?

Choose a crystal that connects you to your crown chakra, like sugilite, opal, amethyst, kyanite, clear quartz, celestite, or apophyllite. Hold your crystal in your palms and bring your hands into prayer or namaste. Slowly raise your palms above your head, reaching toward the sky. Gaze up at them, and then close your eyes and feel the expanse of the universe. We are a part of a much greater whole. Write down the ways in which Sahasrara helps connect you to the *something more* we all feel.

_____

_____

_____

_____

_____

_____

_____

_____

_____

_____

_____

_____

_____

_____

_____

_____

✴ • • • ✴ • • • • • ★ • ✴ • • • ✴ • • • • ✴

On the night of the new moon, when the world is at its darkest, consider the ways in which you are a light for those around you. This can be uncomfortable at first, but if you lean into it, you will discover that you have an impact on so many people.

New Moon Meditation.

Use some cleansing scents like lemon or tea tree essential oil, either in a diffuser or blended with a carrier oil. As you breath in their fragrance, meditate on what you need to clear to make way for this new month. What should be swept away?

✴ • • ✴ • • • • ★ • ✴ • • • ✴ • • • ✴

Fill the page with a gratitude list. Don't stop until you've covered every inch of it.
You'll find that you'll need every bit of paper.

_____   _____   _____

_____   _____   _____

_____   _____   _____

_____   _____   _____

_____   _____   _____

_____   _____   _____

_____   _____   _____

_____   _____   _____

_____   _____   _____

_____   _____   _____

_____   _____   _____

_____   _____   _____

_____   _____   _____

_____   _____   _____

_____   _____   _____

_____   _____   _____

_____   _____   _____

_____   _____   _____

_____   _____   _____

Write a list of the things you enjoy. Knitting, reading, cooking, jogging, yoga, calling a friend, drinking tea, taking a bath. Turn to this list whenever you're feeling a little down and need an idea, a way to boost your day.

Write a kind of family constellation. Start with your parents, and add in any siblings, partners, children—whatever feels like "family" to you. What roles do each of them play in your life? What roles do you serve, in theirs?

Crescent Meditation.

Use some energizing scents like thyme or mint essential oil, either directly on the skin or in a diffuser. Use their energy as you meditate on what you would like to grow this month. What will you cultivate?

Write an imaginary conversation with someone. It can be someone who inspires you, someone you love who has passed, a friend you've lost touch with, or even an ex. What would you want to say, and what would you want to hear?

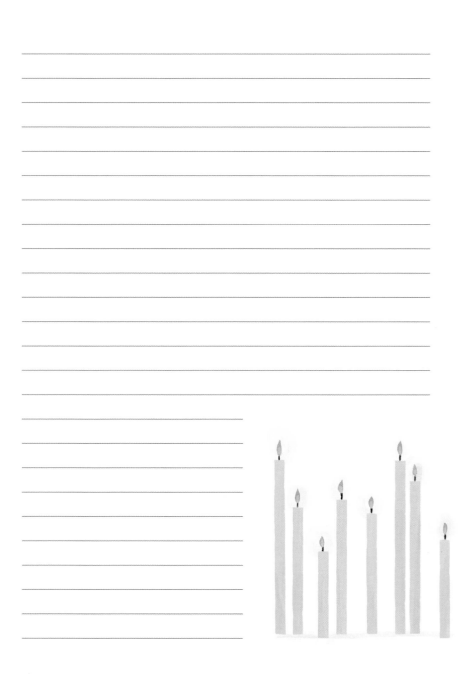

Imagine your life twenty years from now.

What will it look like? Who will you be?

What is something you fear? Write down the moment this fear began—
was it when you were a child? Is it a rational fear? What have you done,
and what can you do, to overcome it?

Gibbous Meditation.

Use jasmine or patchouli essential oils for creativity.
Let your mind wander in this meditation—
if you find yourself daydreaming, go ahead
and give yourself permission to do so, today.
Who knows what you will discover?

What is your earliest memory? It's likely to be fuzzy, and perhaps even a created memory from stories you've been told. But allow yourself some time to explore it—why is this the first thing you remember? What's important about it?

_____

_____

_____

_____

_____

_____

_____

_____

_____

_____

_____

_____

_____

_____

_____

_____

_____

_____

_____

Write a letter to your former self. Comfort yourself for mistakes you made and remember to compliment yourself for the things you are proud of.

Write a letter to your future self. Put everything you wish for her into this letter, writing out your intentions for the person you will become.

Full Moon Meditation.

Use rose or sweet orange essential oils,
to symbolize love and happiness. As you meditate, feel
the love the earth and its little sister the moon
have for you. Feel the power of the gravitational pull
of the moon, and let it bring forth your own power.

What is your favorite myth? These are the stories that have informed who we have become as humans. Make this story your own and retell it here.

_____

_____

_____

_____

_____

_____

_____

_____

_____

_____

_____

_____

_____

_____

_____

_____

_____

_____

_____

_____

_____

_____

_____

Write down your astrological sign, and then look up its shadow, your moon sign. This sign speaks more to your emotional and intuitive nature. How do these two signs complement each other, in you?

_____

_____

_____

_____

_____

_____

_____

_____

_____

_____

_____

_____

_____

_____

_____

_____

_____

_____

_____

_____

_____

_____

_____

Imagine an ancestor. This should be no one you know, but someone many generations back. What is she like? How does her nature support and inform yours? What could you learn from each other?

_____

_____

_____

_____

_____

_____

_____

_____

_____

_____

_____

_____

_____

_____

_____

_____

_____

_____

_____

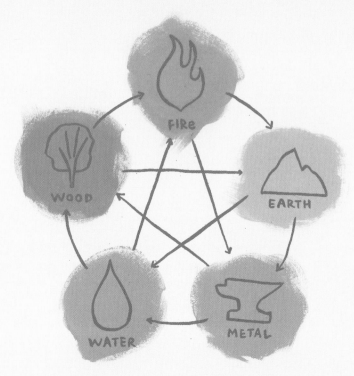

Meditation for the Elements.

Sit cross-legged with your palms face down on your knees. Close your eyes, and begin your meditation with the earth element. Feel your connection with the earth beneath you. Next, turn your attention to your breathing, and feel the air element moving in and out of you. To find the fire element within yourself, simply feel the heat of your palms on your knees. Feel the warmth of your body, and then begin to contemplate the water element. Feel the wetness of your closed eyelids. Imagine the blood pumping through your veins, and recall that you are made almost entirely of water. Finally, hold all of these elements together in your mind, in harmony with one another. Inhale, and exhale.

Do a little research and find a goddess whose nature appeals
to yours. It could be Yemayá, or Hecate, or Ixchel, or Brighid.
Write about what she means to you.

Goddesses are often depicted as Triple Goddesses—the maiden, the mother, and the crone. In what ways do you have this multi-faceted nature? What is the strength of each?

How does the element of air manifest itself in your life?

_____

_____

_____

_____

_____

_____

_____

_____

_____

_____

_____

_____

_____

_____

_____

_____

_____

_____

_____

_____

_____

_____

How does the element of fire manifest itself in your life?

_____

_____

_____

_____

_____

_____

_____

_____

_____

_____

_____

_____

_____

_____

_____

_____

_____

_____

_____

_____

_____

_____

_____

How does the element of earth manifest itself in your life?

_____

_____

_____

_____

_____

_____

_____

_____

_____

_____

_____

_____

_____

_____

_____

_____

_____

_____

_____

_____

_____

How does the element of water manifest itself in your life?

_____

_____

_____

_____

_____

_____

_____

_____

_____

_____

_____

_____

_____

_____

_____

_____

_____

_____

_____

_____

_____

Tea to Enhance Your Psychic Powers.

Create a blend of yarrow, wormwood, rosemary, mugwort, and lavender—you will need a teaspoon's worth for a cup of tea. Pour just-boiled water over your tea strainer, and allow it to steep for ten minutes. Stir in some honey and inhale the fragrance of the herbs as you sip. Write down any impressions you receive.

Lie on the grass and watch the clouds go by. What shapes do you see? What do they mean for you?

_____

_____

_____

_____

_____

_____

_____

_____

_____

_____

_____

_____

_____

_____

_____

_____

_____

_____

_____

_____

_____

_____

What is your favorite flower, and why is it meaningful for you?
What does that say about who you are?

What is your favorite animal, and why is it meaningful for you?
What do you have in common with this animal?

Sigil Magic.

Sigils are powerful forms of intention magic, and
they are both easy and fun to create. Start by writing
down something you want, like "I will fall in love."
Take the first letter of each word and lay them over
each other as you draw them. Then embellish them,
distort them until the letters are hidden from you—and
from prying eyes. You can keep your sigil tucked away,
or turn it into a piece of art.